THE 30-MINUTE SHAKESPEARE
TWELFTH NIGHT

"Nick Newlin's work as a teaching artist for Folger Education during the past thirteen years has provided students, regardless of their experience with Shakespeare or being on stage, a unique opportunity to tread the boards at the Folger Theatre. Working with students to edit Shakespeare's plays for performance at the annual Folger Shakespeare Festivals has enabled students to gain new insights into the Bard's plays, build their skills of comprehension and critical reading, and just plain have fun working collaboratively with their peers.

Folger Education promotes performance-based teaching of Shakespeare's plays, providing students with an interactive approach to Shakespeare's plays in which they participate in a close reading of the text through intellectual, physical, and vocal engagement. Newlin's *The 30-Minute Shakespeare* series is an invaluable resource for teachers of Shakespeare, and for all who are interested in performing the plays."

ROBERT YOUNG, PH.D.
DIRECTOR OF EDUCATION
FOLGER SHAKESPEARE LIBRARY

Twelfth Night: The 30-Minute Shakespeare
ISBN 978-1-935550-04-4
Adaptation, essays, and notes © 2010 by Nick Newlin

Cover design by Sarah Juckniess
Printed in the United States of America

Distributed by Consortium Book Sales & Distribution
www.cbsd.com

NICOLO WHIMSEY PRESS
www.30MinuteShakespeare.com

Art Director: Sarah Juckniess
Managing Editor: Katherine Little

TWELFTH NIGHT
or WHAT YOU WILL

THE 30-MINUTE SHAKESPEARE

Written by WILLIAM SHAKESPEARE

Abridged AND Edited
by NICK NEWLIN

Nicolo Whimsey
Press

Brandywine, MD

To Joanne
My muse
My merry wife

Special thanks to Joanne Flynn, Bill Newlin, Eliza Newlin Carney, William and Louisa Newlin, Michael Tolaydo, Hilary Kacser, Sarah Juckniess, Katherine Little, Eva Zimmerman, Julie Schaper and all of Consortium, Leo Bowman and the students, faculty, and staff at Banneker Academic High School, and Robert Young Ph.D., and the Folger Shakespeare Library, especially the wonderful Education Department.

✳ **TABLE OF CONTENTS**

✳ NO EXPERIENCE NECESSARY

I was not a big "actor type" in high school, so if you weren't either, or if the young people you work with are not, then this book is for you. Whether or not you work with "actor types," you can use this book to stage a lively and captivating thirty-minute version of a Shakespeare play. No experience is necessary.

When I was about eleven years old, my parents took me to see Shakespeare's *Two Gentlemen of Verona*, which was being performed as a Broadway musical. I didn't comprehend every word I heard, but I was enthralled with the language, the characters, and the story, and I understood enough of it to follow along. From then on, I associated Shakespeare with *fun*.

Of course Shakespeare is fun. The Elizabethan audiences knew it, which is one reason he was so popular. It didn't matter that some of the language eluded them. The characters were passionate and vibrant, and their conflicts were compelling. Young people study Shakespeare in high school, but more often than not they read his work like a text book and then get quizzed on academic elements of the play, such as plot, theme, and vocabulary. These are all very interesting, but not nearly as interesting as standing up and performing a scene! It is through performance that the play comes alive and all its "academic" elements are revealed. There is nothing more satisfying to a student or teacher than the feeling of "owning" a Shakespeare play, and that can only come from performing it.

But Shakespeare's plays are often two or more hours long, making the performance of an entire play almost out of the question. One can perform a single scene, which is certainly a good start, but what about the story? What about the changes a character goes through as the play progresses? When school groups perform one scene unedited, or when they lump several plays together, the audience can get lost. This is why I have always preferred to tell the story of the play.

The 30-Minute Shakespeare gives students and teachers a chance to get up on their feet and act out a Shakespeare play in half an hour, using his language. The emphasis is on key scenes, with narrative bridges between scenes to keep the audience caught up on the action. The stage directions are built into this script so that young actors do not have to stand in one place; they can move and tell the story with their actions as well as their words. And it can all be done in a classroom during class time!

That is where this book was born: not in a research library, a graduate school lecture, a professional stage, or even an after-school drama club. All of the play cuttings in *The 30-Minute Shakespeare* were first rehearsed in a D.C. public high school English class, and performed successfully at the Folger Shakespeare Library's annual Secondary School Shakespeare Festival. The players were not necessarily "actor types." For many of them, this was their first performance in a play.

Something almost miraculous happens when students perform Shakespeare. They "get" it. By occupying the characters and speaking the words out loud, students gain a level of understanding and appreciation that is unachievable by simply reading the text. That is the magic of a performance-based method of learning Shakespeare, and this book makes the formerly daunting task of staging a Shakespeare play possible for anybody.

With *The 30-Minute Shakespeare* book series I hope to help teachers and students produce a Shakespeare play in a short amount of time, thus jump-starting the process of discovering the beauty, magic, and fun of the Bard. Plot, theme, and language reveal themselves through the performance of these half-hour play cuttings, and everybody involved receives the priceless gift of "owning" a piece of Shakespeare. The result is an experience that is fun and engaging, and one that we can all carry with us as we play out our own lives on the stages of the world.

NICK NEWLIN
Brandywine, MD
March 2010

CHARACTERS IN THE PLAY

The following is a list of characters that appear in this cutting of
Twelfth Night.

*Twenty-three actors performed in the original production. This
number can be increased to about thirty or decreased to about
twelve by having actors share or double roles.*

For the full breakdown of characters, see Sample Program.

FESTE: Jester to Countess Olivia

MARIA: Olivia's waiting gentlewoman

OLIVIA: An Illyrian countess

VIOLA: A lady of Messaline shipwrecked on the coast of Illyria
(disguised as Cesario)

MALVOLIO: Steward in Olivia's household

ORSINO: Duke of Illyria

CURIO: Gentleman serving Orsino

SIR TOBY BELCH: Olivia's kinsman

SIR ANDREW AGUECHEEK: Sir Toby's companion

ATTENDANTS

MUSICIANS

NARRATORS

✳ SCENE 1. (ACT I, SCENE V)

Olivia's house.

STAGEHANDS *set bench stage right, chair stage left, and table center stage.*

Enter **NARRATOR** *from stage rear.*

As **NARRATOR** *introduces the roles, players enter from stage rear, cross the stage in character, and exit stage right (see Performance Notes).*

NARRATOR
> Our story takes place in Illyria, an ancient (and mythical) country in Southern Europe on the Adriatic Sea. Two twins, Sebastian and Viola are separated in a shipwreck. Viola, believing her brother Sebastian to be dead, disguises herself as a man and takes a position as a page in the Court of the Duke Orsino, who is romantically pursuing the wealthy Countess Olivia, still mourning the sudden death of her brother. Living at Olivia's household is her drunken cousin Sir Toby, with frequent visits by his goofy party friend Sir Andrew Aguecheek. Also at Olivia's house are the puritanical and fun-hating Malvolio, the maid, Maria, and the court Fool, who comes and goes as he pleases, Feste: So, our tale begins, with Viola being sent to Olivia's estate to deliver a love message from the Duke Orsino, *(whispering to audience)* whom Viola herself secretly loves. The scene takes place in the courtyard of the estate of Countess Olivia.

Exit NARRATOR *stage rear.*

FESTE, *stage right, by bench, is practicing balancing a broom on his chin. Enter* MARIA *from stage rear. When she enters,* FESTE *gives a surprised yelp, and the broom drops.*

MARIA *(takes the broom from the ground and sweeps under the table and chair)*
Tell me where thou hast been!
My lady will hang thee for thy absence.

FESTE
Let her hang me: he that is well hang'd in this world need to fear no colours.

MARIA
That may you be bold to say in your foolery.
(sweeps FESTE'S *shoes playfully)*

FESTE
Well, God give them wisdom that have it; and those that are fools, let them use their talents. *(juggles, center stage, and bows to audience)*

MARIA
Peace, you rogue, no more o' that. Here comes my lady: make your excuse wisely, you were best.
(places the broom against the table)

Exit MARIA *stage rear.*

FESTE *(looking upward)*
Wit, an't be thy will, put me into good fooling!
(winks at audience)

Enter LADY OLIVIA *stage left with* ATTENDANTS *behind her and*

MALVOLIO *bringing up the rear.* OLIVIA *sits in stage left chair,* MALVOLIO *stands to her right, and* ATTENDANTS *stand on either side of the table.*

FESTE *(with a big bow and flourish of his hat)*
>God bless thee, lady!

OLIVIA *(to* MALVOLIO*)*
>Take the fool away.

MALVOLIO *starts to take* FESTE'S *arm, but the latter nimbly escapes, spins around, and lands on the bench in a cross-legged pose, smiling cleverly.*

FESTE
>The lady bade take away the fool; therefore, I say again, take her away.

OLIVIA
>Sir, I bade them take away you.

FESTE
>Lady, I wear not motley in my brain. Good madonna, give me leave to prove you a fool.

OLIVIA
>Make your proof.

FESTE *(approaches the chair and kneels at* OLIVIA'S *feet)*
>Good madonna, why mourn'st thou?

OLIVIA
>Good fool, for my brother's death.

FESTE
>I think his soul is in hell, madonna.

OLIVIA

> I know his soul is in heaven, fool.

FESTE

> The more fool, madonna, to mourn for your brother's soul being in heaven. Take away the fool, gentlemen.

FESTE *stands, puts the fool's cap on* OLIVIA'S *head, pauses, and puts it on* MALVOLIO'S *head instead. He begins to lead* MALVOLIO *out, stage right, but the latter realizes what is happening and indignantly pushes* FESTE *away.* FESTE *tumbles over backward, spins around the stage right pole, and finishes leaning against the pole, smiling.* MALVOLIO *stiffly assumes his position at* OLIVIA'S *right, and she cracks a small smile at this foolery.*

OLIVIA

> What think you of this fool, Malvolio? Doth he not mend?

MALVOLIO

> Yes, and shall do till the pangs of death shake him. Infirmity, that decays the wise, doth ever make the better fool.

FESTE

> God send you, sir, a speedy infirmity, for the better increasing your folly! *(begins to balance the broom on his chin again)*

OLIVIA

> How say you to that, Malvolio?

MALVOLIO

> I marvel your ladyship takes delight in such a barren rascal.

MALVOLIO *crosses to* FESTE *and casts the broom across the room with his cane, knocking* FESTE *to the ground in the process.* FESTE *shoots him a dirty look.*

>Look you now, he's out of his guard already.

ATTENDANT *picks up the broom, casually sweeping a little dust toward* MALVOLIO, *places it at the side of the table, and resumes her position.*

OLIVIA
>O, you are sick of self love, Malvolio.

Exit MALVOLIO *stage right, cocking his ear as if hearing a knock at the door.*

>*(calling after the departing* MALVOLIO*)* There is no slander in an allow'd fool, though he do nothing but rail.

FESTE *(regains his composure and grasps the broom once more, dancing around the room)*
>Now Mercury endue thee with leasing, for thou speak'st well of fools!

Exit FESTE *stage right, still dancing with the broom. Enter* MALVOLIO *stage right, passing the dancing* FESTE *and giving him a dirty look.* FESTE *sweeps the feet and pants of* MALVOLIO, *who hurries away, indignant, and takes his place at* OLIVIA'S *right.*

MALVOLIO
>Madam, there is at the gate a young gentleman much desires to speak with you. What is to be said to him, lady? He's fortified against any denial.

OLIVIA
> Tell him he shall not speak with me.

MALVOLIO
> Has been told so.

OLIVIA
> What kind o' man is he?

MALVOLIO
> Why, of mankind.

OLIVIA
> Of what personage and years is he?

MALVOLIO
> Not yet old enough for a man, nor young enough
> for a boy; one would think his mother's milk were
> scarce out of him.

OLIVIA
> Let him approach: call in my gentlewoman.

MALVOLIO *(calling toward curtain)*
> Gentlewoman, my lady calls.

Exit MALVOLIO *stage right.*

Enter MARIA *from curtain.*

OLIVIA *stands and crosses to table, facing the audience.*
ATTENDANTS *brush her hair and hold the mirror as she applies
her lipstick.*

OLIVIA

> Give me my veil: come, throw it o'er my face.
> We'll once more hear Orsino's embassy.

MARIA *places* OLIVIA'S *veil over her face and then dons her own,
as do the* ATTENDANTS. *They all stand in a line in front of the chair.*

Enter VIOLA, *clutching in her hand a rolled up scroll of paper
tied with a ribbon. She is confused by the ladies, approaches
them, sits on the bench, stands, and tentatively approaches
them again.*

VIOLA

> The honourable lady of the house, which is she?

OLIVIA

> Speak to me; I shall answer for her. Your will?

VIOLA *(reading from her paper)*

> Most radiant, exquisite, and unmatchable beauty,
> *(stops reading)* I pray you, tell me if this be the lady
> of the house, for I never saw her: I would be loathe
> to cast away my speech.

OLIVIA

> What are you? What would you?

VIOLA

> What I am, and what I would, are as secret as
> maidenhead: to your ears, divinity; to any other's,
> profanation. *(looks at* ATTENDANTS *and motions with
> her head for them to leave)*

OLIVIA

> Give us the place alone: we will hear this divinity.

Exit MARIA *and* ATTENDANTS *stage rear.*

VIOLA

Good madam, let me see your face.

OLIVIA *(moves toward the table and takes a quick peek at
the mirror)*

You are now out of your text: but we will draw the
curtain, and show you the picture. *(removes her veil)*
Look you, sir, such a one I was, this present: is't not
well done?

VIOLA *(with a look of admiration, and perhaps some envy
or disappointment)*

Excellently done, if God did all.

OLIVIA

'Tis in grain, sir; 'twill endure wind and weather.

VIOLA

My lord and master loves you.

OLIVIA

How does he love me?

VIOLA

With adorations, with fertile tears,
With groans that thunder love, with sighs of fire.

OLIVIA

Your lord does know my mind; I cannot love him.
(returns to her chair, and sits)

VIOLA

If I did love you in my master's flame,

With such a suffering, such a deadly life,
In your denial I would find no sense;
I would not understand it.

OLIVIA

Why, what would you?

VIOLA *(strolls to the stage right pole, leans against it, and gazes*
out toward the audience)
Make me a willow cabin at your gate,
And call upon my soul within the house;
Write loyal cantons of contemned love,
And sing them loud even in the dead of night;
Halloo your name to the reverberate hills,
And make the babbling gossip of the air
Cry out, "Olivia!"

OLIVIA *(stands up from chair and moves slowly and somewhat*
seductively toward **VIOLA**, *backing her into the*
stage right pole)
You might do much. What is your parentage?

VIOLA

Above my fortunes, yet my state is well: *(clears her*
throat and tries to speak in a lower, more
masculine voice)
I am a gentleman.

OLIVIA

Get you to your lord;
I cannot love him: let him send no more;
Unless, perchance, you come to me again,
To tell me how he takes it. Fare you well:
I thank you for your pains: spend this for me.
(gives her a large coin)

VIOLA

> I am no fee'd post, lady; keep your purse: *(starts to*
> *leave stage right, stops, and turns back)*
> My master, not myself, lacks recompense.
> Farewell, fair cruelty.

Exit VIOLA *stage right.*

OLIVIA *(walking excitedly in a semicircle toward the table,*
> *stopping to inspect herself in the mirror)*
> Thy tongue, thy face, thy limbs, actions, and spirit,
> Do give thee fivefold blazon: not too fast;
> *(stops center stage to keep herself in check)*
> Soft, soft!
> Even so quickly may one catch the plague?
> *(catches her breath, leaning against the table for*
> *support; takes a sip of wine, fans herself, looks*
> *at the wine glass, then drains it in one gulp)*
> Methinks I feel this youth's perfections
> With an invisible and subtle stealth
> To creep in at mine eyes. Well, let it be.
> What, ho, Malvolio!

Enter MALVOLIO *stage right.*

MALVOLIO

> Here, madam, at your service.

OLIVIA

> Run after that same peevish messenger,
> The county's man: he left this ring behind him,
> If that the youth will come this way to-morrow,
> I'll give him reasons for't. *(hands him the ring)*
> Hie thee, Malvolio.

MALVOLIO
>   Madam, I will.

Exit MALVOLIO *stage right.*

OLIVIA *(facing front)*
>   I do I know not what; and fear to find
>   Mine eye too great a flatterer for my mind.
>   Fate, show thy force: ourselves we do not owe;
>   What is decreed must be, and be this so!

Exit OLIVIA, *quickly, stage left.*

STAGEHANDS *remove bench, place chair stage right, bring on throne and place it to the right of chair, and place table stage left, setting it with wine bottle, glasses, and a plate of fruit*

Enter NARRATOR *from stage rear.*

✳ SCENE 2. (ACT II, SCENE IV)

Duke Orsino's palace.

NARRATOR

Back at Duke Orsino's palace, the Duke has a "man to man" talk with Viola about men's passions, as Viola struggles to keep her own feelings for the Duke secret.

Exit **NARRATOR** *stage rear.*

Enter **DUKE ORSINO, VIOLA,** *and* **CURIO** *from stage left. Enter* **DUKE ORSINO'S BAND** *from stage rear, comically playing over one another.* **DUKE ORSINO** *sits in his throne, with* **VIOLA** *in the chair to his left and* **CURIO** *standing to the right of the table.* **CURIO** *offers an apple slice to* **DUKE ORSINO,** *who takes a thoughtful bite and puts the slice back on the tray. The music stops.*

DUKE ORSINO

If Music be the food of love, play on!
Now, good Cesario, but that piece of song,
That old and antique song we heard last night:
Methought it did relieve my passion much,
Come, but one verse.

CURIO

He is not here, so please your lordship, that should
　　　　sing it.

CURIO *offers an apple slice to* **VIOLA,** *who reaches for it then changes her mind. As* **CURIO** *passes by* **BAND,** *a member grabs*

*a slice, and the other members roll their eyes. Before she can
eat it,* CURIO *snatches the slice away, looks around, cleans it off
a bit, and puts it back on the tray. He then takes a bite of fruit
himself, and puts the rest in his pocket.*

DUKE ORSINO
> Who was it?

CURIO *(regaining his composure, trying not to reveal that he has
eaten the fruit)*
> Feste, the jester, my lord; a fool that the Lady Olivia's
> father took much delight in: he is about the house.

DUKE ORSINO
> Seek him out: and play the tune the while.

Exit CURIO *stage left.*

Once again, BAND *begins to play, each member playing over
the other.*

> Come hither, boy: if ever thou shalt love,
> In the sweet pangs of it remember me;
> How dost thou like this tune?

VIOLA
> It gives a very echo to the seat
> Where Love is throned.

VIOLA *leans against* DUKE ORSINO *while the music plays, and
both feel a strange sense of discomfort. The music stops.*

DUKE ORSINO *(regains his composure)*
> Thou dost speak masterly:
> My life upon't, young though thou art, thine eye

> Hath stay'd upon some favour that it loves;
> Hath it not, boy?

VIOLA

> A little, by your favour.

DUKE ORSINO

> What kind of woman is't?

VIOLA

> Of your complexion.

VIOLA moves her chair closer to his, beginning to lean against him, when they are surprised.

Enter CURIO and FESTE from stage rear.

DUKE ORSINO

> O, fellow, come, the song we had last night.
> It is old and plain,
> And dallies with the innocence of love,
> Like the old age.

FESTE

> Are you ready, sir?

DUKE ORSINO

> Ay; prithee, sing.

BAND MEMBER is about to get her chance for a solo, and there is a silence as she takes time to prepare. She triumphantly blows one note, but it is interrupted by a sudden whistle from FESTE. Enter DRUMMERS stage right, followed by other members of FESTE'S BAND. ALL dance and move to the music, with DUKE ORSINO'S BAND eventually joining in.

FESTE *(with singers repeating certain words)*
> Come away, come away, death,
> And in sad cypress let me be laid;
> Fly away, fly away, breath;
> I am slain by a fair cruel maid.
> My shroud of white, stuck all with yew,
> O, prepare it!
> My part of death, no one so true
> Did share it.
> Not a flower, not a flower sweet,
> On my black coffin let there be strown;
> Not a friend, not a friend greet
> My poor corpse, where my bones shall be thrown:
> A thousand thousand sighs to save,
> Lay me, O, where
> Sad true lover never find my grave,
> To weep there!

Exit FESTE, SINGERS, BANDS, *and* CURIO *stage right, all dancing and drumming.* DUKE ORSINO *and* VIOLA *look on amusedly. They are alone now.*

VIOLA
> My Lord,
> Say that some lady, as perhaps there is,
> Hath for your love as great a pang of heart
> As you have for Olivia . . .

DUKE ORSINO
> There is no woman's sides
> Can bide the beating of so strong a passion
> As love doth give my heart; no woman's heart
> So big, to hold so much. Make no compare
> Between that love a woman can bear me
> And that I owe Olivia.

VIOLA *(crosses to the table and sneaks a look at herself in her*
pocket mirror)
Ay, but I know—

DUKE ORSINO
What dost thou know?

VIOLA *(turns to face him; walks slightly forward, center stage)*
Too well what love women to men may owe:
In faith, they are as true of heart as we.
My father had a daughter loved a man,
As it might be, perhaps, were I a woman,
I should your lordship. *(throws him a coy, sidelong*
glance)

DUKE ORSINO
And what's her history?

VIOLA *(turns her head away from him again; speaks out to*
audience)
A blank, my lord. She never told her love.
And, with a green and yellow melancholy,
She sat like Patience on a monument,
Smiling at grief. *(turns to him)* Was not this love indeed?
We men may say more, swear more: but, indeed,
Our shows are more than will; for still we prove
Much in our vows, but little in our love.

DUKE ORSINO *(walks sympathetically toward* **VIOLA** *and puts his*
arm around her shoulder)
But died thy sister of her love, my boy?

VIOLA *(liking his touch but also finding it hard to bear; pulls*
away, turns, and takes a step forward)
I am all the daughters of my father's house,

And all the brothers too; and yet I know not.
(pauses; turns back to him)
Sir, shall I to this lady?

DUKE ORSINO
Ay, that's the theme.
To her in haste; give her this jewel; say,
My love can give no place, bide no delay.

Exit VIOLA *stage right and* DUKE ORSINO *stage rear, both stopping to look back at each other as they leave.*

STAGEHANDS *remove throne, move table to center stage, and place two more chairs around the table, setting it with two mugs (one large and one small), bottle of wine, pot, pan, and two wooden spoons.*

Enter NARRATOR *from stage rear.*

✳ SCENE 3. (ACT II, SCENE III)

Olivia's house.

NARRATOR
> Meanwhile, back at Olivia's house, Sir Toby,
> Sir Andrew, and Feste sing and dance the night
> away. This does not sit well with Malvolio.

Exit **NARRATOR** *stage rear.*

Enter **SIR TOBY BELCH** *and* **SIR ANDREW AGUECHEEK** *from stage rear.* **SIR TOBY** *immediately fills the huge mug for himself and the small one for his companion. He takes a center stage seat.*

SIR TOBY BELCH
> Approach, Sir Andrew: not to be a-bed after
> midnight is to be up betimes. *(hands the small cup
> to* **SIR ANDREW**, *who examines his meager portion)*

SIR ANDREW AGUECHEEK *(sits in stage right chair)*
> I know not: but I know, to be up late is to be up late.
> *(clink their mugs and drink to that)*

SIR TOBY BELCH
> A false conclusion: I hate it as an unfill'd can. *(holds
> up empty wine bottle and tries to shake out its last
> few drops)* To be up after midnight, and to go to bed
> then, is early; let us therefore eat and drink. *(calls to
> stage left door)* Maria, I say! A stoup of wine! *(waves
> the empty bottle about, attempting to suck out more
> liquid, somehow)*

SIR ANDREW AGUECHEEK

> Here comes the fool, i' faith.

Enter FESTE *from stage right.*

SIR ANDREW *spots* FESTE, *who motions for him to be quiet as he taps* SIR TOBY *on his right shoulder, then his left, and hides behind the chair. He peers over the top of the chair, surprising* SIR TOBY, *who gives a whoop and nearly jumps out of his seat.*

FESTE

> How now, my hearts! Did you never see the picture
> of We Three?

FESTE *puts his arm around the two men and produces a flask from his pocket, which delights* SIR TOBY. *He sits in stage right chair.*

SIR TOBY BELCH

> Welcome, ass. Now let's have a catch.

SIR ANDREW AGUECHEEK

> By my troth, the fool has an excellent breast.
> Now, a song.

SIR TOBY *reaches into his own purse, which is empty, so he reaches into* SIR ANDREW'S, *who doesn't even notice.* SIR TOBY *hands a coin to* FESTE.

SIR TOBY BELCH

> Come on; there is sixpence for you: let's have a song.

FESTE

> Would you have a love-song, or a song of good life?

SIR TOBY BELCH

> A love-song, a love-song.

SIR ANDREW AGUECHEEK
Ay, ay: I care not for good life.

FESTE *gives a flourish and a whistle, and* FESTE'S BAND *enters noisily to see what the commotion is about. Once the disorder dies down,* SINGERS *perform the song, standing between* FESTE *and* TOBY, *slightly upstage.*

SINGERS
O mistress mine, where are you roaming?
O, stay and hear; your true-love's coming,
That can sing both high and low:
Trip no further, pretty sweeting;
Journeys end in lovers' meeting,
Every wise man's son doth know.
What is love? 'Tis not hereafter;
Present mirth hath present laughter;
What's to come is still unsure:
In delay there lies no plenty;
Then come kiss me, sweet-and-twenty,
Youth's a stuff will not endure.

SINGERS *curtsy coyly to the men as* MARIA *grabs one of the wine jugs for them to share. Exit* SINGERS *and* MARIA *stage left.*

SIR ANDREW AGUECHEEK *(leaning on his elbows, his face close to* SIR TOBY'S, *gazing fondly toward where the women once were)*
A mellifluous voice, as I am true knight.

SIR TOBY BELCH *(smells his breath and falls back in his chair)*
A contagious breath.

SIR ANDREW AGUECHEEK *(not realizing* SIR TOBY *is referring to his breath)*
Very sweet and contagious, i' faith.

SIR TOBY BELCH

> To hear by the nose, it is dulcet in contagion.
> But shall we make the welkin dance indeed?

SIR ANDREW AGUECHEEK

> Most certain. Let our catch be, "Thou knave."
> Begin, fool: it begins, "Hold thy peace."

FESTE

> I shall never begin, if I hold my peace.

SIR ANDREW AGUECHEEK

> Good, i' faith. Come, begin.

They all stand and sing the song, accompanied by **FESTE'S BAND**,
and dance around the table banging pots and pans, singing,
"Hold thy peace, Thou Knave,—Huh! Hold thy peace!"

Enter **MARIA** *stage right.*

MARIA

> What a caterwauling do you keep here! If my lady
> have not call'd up her steward Malvolio, and bid him
> turn you out of doors, never trust me.

SIR TOBY BELCH

> Tilly-vally, lady! *(sings)* "There dwelt a man in
> Babylon, lady, lady!"

SIR ANDREW, FESTE, *and* **FESTE'S BAND** *join in, repeating* "*Lady*
lady," and the noise level rises again.

MARIA

> For the love o' God, peace!

Enter **MALVOLIO** *from stage rear. He is dressed in a ridiculous*
nightshirt, nightcap, and slippers.

MALVOLIO

My masters, are you mad? Or what are you? Have
you no wit, manners, nor honesty, but to gabble
like tinkers at this time of night? Do ye make an
ale-house of my lady's house? Is there no respect of
place, persons, nor time, in you?

SIR TOBY BELCH

We did keep time, sir, in our catches. Sneck-up!
(offers his mug to MALVOLIO, *who recoils
in disgust)*

MALVOLIO

Sir Toby, I must be round with you. My lady bade
me tell you, that, though she harbours you as her
kinsman, she's nothing allied to your disorders.

DRUMMERS *start up again.*

SIR TOBY BELCH *(sings)*

Shall I bid him go?

FESTE *(sings)*

What an if you do?

SIR TOBY BELCH *(sings)*

Shall I bid him go, and spare not?

FESTE *(sings)*

O, no, no, no, no, you dare not.

MALVOLIO *takes a drumstick from* DRUMMER *and breaks it.*
DRUMMER *immediately produces another drumstick from his
jacket pocket.*

SIR TOBY BELCH *(walks right into* **MALVOLIO'S** *face)*
> Out o' time, sir? Ye lie. Art any more than a steward?
> Dost thou think, because thou art virtuous, there
> shall be no more cakes and ale? Go, sir, rub your
> chain with crumbs. A stoup of wine, Maria!

MALVOLIO *(takes a step toward curtain and turns around)*
> Mistress Mary, if you prized my lady's favour at
> any thing more than contempt, you would not give
> means for this uncivil rule: she shall know of it, by
> this hand.

Exit **MALVOLIO** *stage rear.*

MARIA *(calling after him)*
> Go shake your ears!

ALL *join in with a rousing chorus of, "Go shake your ears! Go shake your ears!"*

SIR TOBY BELCH
> Come, Come. I'll go burn some sack; 'tis too late to
> go to bed now.

Drums start softly as a prelude to singing of the last song.

Enter **NARRATOR** *from stage right, coming downstage.*

NARRATOR
> In time, Viola's twin brother Sebastian reappears
> alive and well,

Enter **VIOLA** *from stage right (as Sebastian) with her hair still up.*

> and marries the happy Olivia,

Enter **OLIVIA** *from stage left; she dances with* **VIOLA** *(as Sebastian).*

and the Duke Orsino finds love with the ecstatic Viola.

VIOLA *turns around, lets down her hair, spins back around, and dances with* DUKE ORSINO, *who has entered from stage right.*

Sir Toby and Maria even get married!

SIR TOBY *and* MARIA *dance.*

What a life! And, even though there is still some ill will between Malvolio and the revelers, for the end of our merry play, we invited him to join in the dance too!

Enter MALVOLIO *from stage rear, who stands stiffly with arms crossed, scowling, and then gradually begins to smile and dance a little.*

Enter ALL, *dancing.*

ALL *(singing "The Wind and the Rain")*
    When that I was and a little tiny boy,
    With hey, ho, the wind and the rain,
    A foolish thing was but a toy,
    For the rain it raineth every day.

    But when I came to man's estate,
    With hey, ho, the wind and the rain,
    'Gainst knaves and thieves men shut their gate,
    For the rain it raineth every day.

    But when I came, alas, to wive,
    With hey, ho, the wind and the rain
    By swaggering could I never thrive,
    For the rain it raineth every day.

But when I came unto my beds,
With hey, ho, the wind and the rain,
With tosspots still had drunken heads,
For the rain it raineth every day.

A great while ago the world begun,
With hey, ho, the wind and the rain,
But that's all one, our play is done,
And we'll strive to please you every day

And we'll strive to please you every day.

All hold hands and take a bow. Exeunt.

✳ PERFORMING SHAKESPEARE

HOW *THE 30-MINUTE SHAKESPEARE* WAS BORN

In 1981 I performed a "Shakespeare Juggling" piece called "To Juggle or Not To Juggle" at the first Folger Library Secondary School Shakespeare Festival. The audience consisted of about 200 Washington, D.C. area high school students who had just performed thirty-minute versions of Shakespeare plays for each other and were jubilant over the experience. I was dressed in a jester's outfit, and my job was to entertain them. I juggled and jested and played with Shakespeare's words, notably Hamlet's "To be or not to be" soliloquy, to very enthusiastic response. I was struck by how much my "Shakespeare Juggling" resonated with a group who had just performed Shakespeare themselves. "Getting" Shakespeare is a heady feeling, especially for adolescents, and I am continually delighted at how much joy and satisfaction young people derive from performing Shakespeare. Simply reading and studying this great playwright does not even come close to inspiring the kind of enthusiasm that comes from performance.

Surprisingly, many of these students were not "actor types." A good percentage of the students performing Shakespeare that day were part of an English class which had rehearsed the plays during class time. Fifteen years later, when I first started directing plays in D.C. public schools as a Teaching Artist with the Folger Shakespeare Library, I entered a ninth grade English class as a guest and spent two or three days a week for two or three months preparing students for the Folger's annual Secondary School Shakespeare Festival. I have conducted this annual residency with the Folger ever since. Every year for seven action-packed days, eight groups of students between grades seven and twelve tread the boards onstage at the Folger's Elizabethan Theatre, a grand recreation of a sixteenth-century venue with a three-tiered gallery, carved oak columns, and a sky-painted canopy.

As noted on the Folger website (www.folger.edu), "The festival is a celebration of the Bard, not a competition. Festival commentators—drawn from the professional theater and Shakespeare education communities—recognize exceptional performances, student directors, and good spirit amongst the students with selected awards at the end of each day. They are also available to share feedback with the students."

My annual Folger Teaching Artist engagement, directing a Shakespeare play in a public high school English class, is the most challenging and the most rewarding thing I do all year. I hope this book can bring you the same rewards.

GETTING STARTED

GAMES

How can you get an English class (or any other group of young people, or even adults) to start the seemingly daunting task of performing a Shakespeare play? You have already successfully completed the critical first step, which is buying this book. You hold in your hand a performance-ready, thirty-minute cutting of a Shakespeare play, with stage directions to get the actors moving about the stage purposefully. But it's a good idea to warm the group up with some theater games.

One good initial exercise is called "Positive/Negative Salutations." Students stand in two lines facing each other (four or five students in each line) and, reading from index cards, greet each other, first with a "Positive" salutation in Shakespeare's language (using actual phrases from the plays), followed by a "negative" greeting.

Additionally, short vocal exercises are an essential part of the preparation process. The following is a very simple and effective vocal warm-up: Beginning with the number two, have the whole group count to twenty using increments of two (i.e., "Two, four, six . . ."). Increase the volume slightly with each number, reaching top volume with "twenty," and then decrease the volume while counting back down, so that the students are practically whispering when they arrive again at "two." This exercise teaches dynamics and allows them to get loud as a group without any individual pressure. Frequently during a rehearsal period, if a student is mumbling inaudibly, I will refer back to this exercise as a reminder that we can and often do belt it out!

"Stomping Words" is a game that is very helpful at getting a handle on Shakespeare's rhythm. Choose a passage in iambic pentameter and have the group members walk around the room in a circle, stomping their feet on the second beat of each line:

Two **house**-holds, **both** a-**like** in **dig**-nity
In **fair** Ve-**ro**na **Where** we **lay** our **scene**

Do the same thing with a prose passage, and have the students discuss their experience with it, including points at which there is an extra beat, etc., and what, if anything, it might signify.

I end every vocal warm-up with a group reading of one of the speeches from the play, emphasizing diction and projection, bouncing off consonants, and encouraging the group members to listen to each other so that they can speak the lines together in unison. For variety I will throw in some classic "tongue twisters" too, such as, "The sixth sheik's sixth sheep is sick."

The Folger Shakespeare Library's website (http://www.folger.edu) and their book series *Shakespeare Set Free,* edited by Peggy O'Brien, are two great resources for getting started with a performance-based teaching of Shakespeare in the classroom. The Folger website has numerous helpful resources and activities, many submitted by teachers, for helping a class actively participate in the process of getting to know a Shakespeare play. For more simple theater games, Viola Spolin's *Theatre Games for the Classroom* is very helpful, as is one I use frequently, *Theatre Games for Young Performers.*

HATS AND PROPS

Introducing a few hats and props early in the process is a good way to get the action going. Hats, in particular, provide a nice avenue for giving young actors a non-verbal way of getting into character. In the opening weeks, when students are still holding onto their scripts, a hat can give an actor a way to "feel" like a character. Young actors are natural masters at injecting their own personality into what they wear, and even small choices made with how a hat is worn (jauntily, shadily, cockily, mysteriously) provide a starting point for discussion of specific characters, their traits, and their relationships with other characters. All such discussions always lead back to one thing: the text. "Mining the text" is consistently the best strategy for uncovering the mystery of Shakespeare's language. That is where all the answers lie: in the words themselves.

WHAT DO THE WORDS MEAN?

It is essential that young actors know what they are saying when they recite Shakespeare. If not, they might as well be scat singing, riffing on sounds and rhythm but not conveying a specific meaning. The real question is: What do the words mean? The answer is multifaceted, and can be found in more than one place. The New Folger Library paperback editions of the plays themselves (edited by Barbara Mowat and Paul Werstine, Washington Square Press) are a great resource for understanding Shakespeare's words and passages and "translating" them into modern English. These editions also contain chapters on Shakespeare's language, his life, his theater, a "Modern Perspective," and further reading. There is a wealth of scholarship embedded in these wonderful books, and I make it a point to read them cover to cover before embarking on a play-directing project. At the very least, it is a good idea for any adult who intends to direct a Shakespeare play with a group of students to go through the explanatory notes that appear on the pages facing the text. These explanatory notes are an indispensable "translation tool."

The best way to get students to understand what Shakespeare's words mean is to ask them what they think they mean. Students have their own associations with the words and with how they sound and feel. The best ideas on how to perform Shakespeare often come directly from the students, not from anybody else's notion. If a student has an idea or feeling about a word or passage, and it resonates with her emotionally, physically, or spiritually, then Shakespeare's words can be a vehicle for her feelings. That can result in some powerful performances!

I make it my job as director to read the explanatory notes in the Folger text, but I make it clear to the students that almost "anything goes" when trying to understand Shakespeare. There are no wrong interpretations. Students have their own experiences, with some shared and some uniquely their own. If someone has an association with the phrase "canker-blossom," or if the words make that student or his character feel or act a certain way, then that is the "right" way to decipher it.

I encourage the students to refer to the Folger text's explanatory notes and to keep a pocket dictionary handy. Young actors must attach some meaning to every word or line they recite. If I feel an actor is glossing over a word, I will stop him and ask him what he is saying. If he doesn't know, we will figure it out together as a group.

PROCESS VS. PRODUCT

The process of learning Shakespeare by performing one of his plays is more important than whether everybody remembers his lines or whether somebody misses a cue or an entrance. But my Teaching Artist residencies have always had the end goal of a public performance for about 200 other students, so naturally the performance starts to take precedence over the process somewhere around dress rehearsal in the students' minds. It is my job to make sure the actors are prepared— otherwise they will remember the embarrassing moment of a public mistake and not the glorious triumph of owning a Shakespeare play.

In one of my earlier years of play directing, I was sitting in the audience as one of my narrators stood frozen on stage for at least a minute, trying to remember her opening line. I started scrambling in my backpack below my seat for a script, at last prompting her from the audience. Despite her fine performance, that embarrassing moment is all she remembered from the whole experience. Since then I have made sure to assign at least one person to prompt from backstage if necessary. Additionally, I inform the entire cast that if somebody is dying alone out there, it is okay to rescue him or her with an offstage prompt.

There is always a certain amount of stage fright that will accompany a performance, especially a public one for an unfamiliar audience. As a director, I live with stage fright as well, even though I am not appearing on stage. The only antidote to this is work and preparation. If a young actor is struggling with her lines, I make sure to arrange for a session where we run lines over the telephone. I try to set up a buddy system so that students can run lines with their peers, and this often works well. But if somebody does not have a "buddy," I will personally make the time to help out myself. As I assure my students from the outset, I am not going to let them fail or embarrass themselves. They need an experienced leader. And if the leader has experience in teaching but not in directing Shakespeare, then he needs this book!

It is a good idea to culminate in a public performance, as opposed to an in-class project, even if it is only for another classroom. Student actors want to show their newfound Shakespearian thespian skills to an outside group, and this goal motivates them to do a good job. In that respect, "product" is important. Another wonderful bonus to performing a play is that it is a unifying group effort. Students learn teamwork. They learn to give focus to another actor when he is speaking, and to play off of other characters. I like to end each performance with the entire cast reciting a passage in unison. This is a powerful ending, one that reaffirms the unity of the group.

SEEING SHAKESPEARE PERFORMED

It is very helpful for young actors to see Shakespeare performed by a group of professionals, whether they are appearing live on stage (preferable but not always possible) or on film. Because an entire play can take up two or more full class periods, time may be an issue. I am fortunate because thanks to a local foundation that underwrites theater education in the schools, I have been able to take my school groups to a Folger Theatre matinee of the play that they are performing. I always pick a play that is being performed locally that season. But not all group leaders are that lucky. Fortunately, there is the Internet, specifically YouTube. A quick YouTube search for "Shakespeare" can unearth thousands of results, many appropriate for the classroom.

The first "Hamlet" result showed an 18-year-old African-American actor on the streets of Camden, New Jersey, delivering a riveting performance of Hamlet's "The play's the thing." The second clip was from *Cat Head Theatre*, an animation of cats performing Hamlet. Of course, YouTube boasts not just alley cats and feline thespians, but also clips by true legends of the stage, such as John Gielgud and Richard Burton. These clips can be saved and shown in classrooms, providing useful inspiration.

One advantage of the amazing variety of clips available on YouTube is that students can witness the wide range of interpretations for any given scene, speech, or character in Shakespeare, thus freeing them from any preconceived notion that there is a "right" way to do it. Furthermore, modern interpretations of the Bard may appeal to those who are put off by the "thees and thous" of Elizabethan speech.

By seeing Shakespeare performed either live or on film, students are able to hear the cadence, rhythm, vocal dynamics, and pronunciation of the language, and they can appreciate the life that other actors breathe into the characters. They get to see the story told dramatically, which inspires them to tell their own version.

PUTTING IT ALL TOGETHER

THE STEPS

After a few sessions of theater games to warm up the group, it's time to begin the process of casting the play. Each play cutting in *The 30-Minute Shakespeare* series includes a cast list and a sample program, demonstrating which parts have been divided. Cast size is generally between twelve and thirty students, with major roles frequently assigned to more than one performer. In other words, one student may play Juliet in the first scene, another in the second scene, and yet another in the third. This will distribute the parts evenly so that there is no "star of the show." Furthermore, this prevents actors from being burdened with too many lines. If I have an actor who is particularly talented or enthusiastic, I will give her a bigger role. It is important to go with the grain—one cast member's enthusiasm can be contagious.

I provide the performer of each shared role with a similar head-piece and/or cape, so that the audience can keep track of the characters. When there are sets of twins, I try to use blue shirts and red shirts, so that the audience has at least a fighting chance of figuring it out! Other than these costume consistencies, I rely on the text and the audience's observance to sort out the doubling of characters. Generally, the audience can follow because we are telling the story.

Some participants are shy and do not wish to speak at all on stage. To these students I assign non-speaking parts and technical roles such as sound operator and stage manager. However, I always get everybody on stage at some point, even if it is just for the final group speech, because I want every group member to experience what it is like to be on a stage as part of an ensemble.

CASTING THE PLAY

Young people can be self-conscious and nervous with "formal" auditions, especially if they have little or no acting experience.

I conduct what I call an "informal" audition process. I hand out a questionnaire asking students if there is any particular role that they desire, whether they play a musical instrument. To get a feel for them as people, I also ask them to list one or two hobbies or interests. Occasionally this will inform my casting decisions. If someone can juggle, and the play has the part of a Fool, that skill may come in handy. Dancing or martial arts abilities can also be applied to roles.

For the auditions, I do not use the cut script. I have students stand and read from the Folger edition of the complete text in order to hear how they fare with the longer passages. I encourage them to breathe and carry their vocal energy all the way to the end of a long line of text. I also urge them to play with diction, projection, modulation, and dynamics, elements of speech that we have worked on in our vocal warm-ups and theater games.

I base my casting choices largely on reading ability, vocal strength, and enthusiasm for the project. If someone has requested a particular role, I try to honor that request. I explain that even with a small part, an actor can create a vivid character that adds a lot to the play. Wide variations in personality types can be utilized: if there are two students cast as Romeo, one brooding and one effusive, I try to put the more brooding Romeo in an early lovelorn scene, and place the effusive Romeo in the balcony scene. Occasionally one gets lucky, and the doubling of characters provides a way to match personality types with different aspects of a character's personality. But also be aware of the potential serendipity of non-traditional casting. For example, I have had one of the smallest students in the class play a powerful Othello. True power comes from within!

Generally, I have more females than males in a class, so women are more likely (and more willing) to play male characters than vice versa.

Rare is the high school boy who is brave enough to play a female character, which is unfortunate because it can reap hilarious results.

GET OUTSIDE HELP

Every time there is a fight scene in one of the plays I am directing, I call on my friend Michael Tolaydo, a professional actor and theater professor at St. Mary's College, who is an expert in all aspects of theater, including fight choreography. Not only does Michael stage the fight, but he does so in a way that furthers the action of the play, highlighting character's traits and bringing out the best in the student actors. Fight choreography must be done by an expert or somebody could get hurt. In the absence of such help, super slow-motion fights are always a safe bet and can be quite effective, especially when accompanied by a soundtrack on the boom box.

During dress rehearsals I invite my friend Hilary Kacser, a Washington-area actor and dialect coach for two decades. Because I bring her in late in the rehearsal process, I have her direct her comments to me, which I then filter and relay to the cast. This avoids confusing the cast with a second set of directions. This caveat only applies to general directorial comments from outside visitors. Comments on specific artistic disciplines such as dance, music, and stage combat can come from the outside experts themselves.

If you work in a school, you might have helpful resources within your own building, such as a music or dance teacher who could contribute their expertise to a scene. If nobody is available in your school, try seeking out a member of the local professional theater. Many local performing artists will be glad to help, and the students are usually thrilled to have a visit from a professional performer.

LET STUDENTS BRING THEMSELVES INTO THE PLAY

The best ideas often come from the students themselves. If a young actor has a notion of how to play a scene, I will always give that idea a try. In a rehearsal of *Henry IV, Part 1*, one traveler jumped into the other's arms when they were robbed. It got a huge laugh. This was something that they did on instinct. We kept that bit for the performance, and it worked wonderfully.

As a director, you have to foster an environment in which that kind of spontaneity can occur. The students have to feel safe to experiment. In the same production of *Henry IV*, Falstaff and Hal invented a little fist bump "secret handshake" to use in the battle scene. The students were having fun and bringing parts of themselves into the play. Shakespeare himself would have approved. When possible I try to err on the side of fun because if the young actors are having fun, then they will commit themselves to the project. The beauty of the language, the story, the characters, and the pathos will follow.

There is a balance to be achieved here, however. In that same production of *Henry IV, Part 1*, the student who played Bardolph was having a great time with her character. She carried a leather wineskin around and offered it up to the other characters in the tavern. It was a prop with which she developed a comic relationship. At the end of our thirty-minute *Henry IV, Part 1*, I added a scene from *Henry IV, Part 2* as a coda: The new King Henry V (formerly Falstaff's drinking and carousing buddy Hal) rejects Falstaff, banishing him from within ten miles of the King. It is a sad and sobering moment, one of the most powerful in the play.

But at the performance, in the middle of the King's rejection speech (played by a female student, and her only speech), Bardolph offered her flask to King Henry and got a big laugh, thus not only upstaging the King but also undermining the seriousness and poignancy of the whole scene. She did not know any better; she was bringing herself to the character as I had been encouraging her to do. But it was inappropriate, and in subsequent seasons, if I foresaw something like that happening as an individual joyfully occupied a character, I attempted to prevent it. Some things we cannot predict. Now I make sure to issue a statement warning against changing any of the blocking on show day, and to watch out for upstaging one's peers.

FOUR FORMS OF ENGAGEMENT: VOCAL, EMOTIONAL, PHYSICAL, AND INTELLECTUAL

When directing a Shakespeare play with a group of students, I always start with the words themselves because the words have the power to engage the emotions, mind, and body. Also, I start with the words in action, as in the previously mentioned exercise, "Positive and Negative Salutations." Students become physically engaged; their bodies react to the images the words evoke. The words have the power to trigger a switch in both the teller and the listener, eliciting both an emotional and physical reaction. I have never heard a student utter the line "Fie! Fie! You counterfeit, you puppet you!" without seeing him change before my eyes. His spine stiffens, his eyes widen, and his fingers point menacingly.

Having used Shakespeare's words to engage the students emotionally and physically, one can then return to the text for a more reflective discussion of what the words mean to us personally. I always make sure to leave at least a few class periods open for discussion of the text, line by line, to ensure that students understand intellectually what they feel viscerally. The advantage to a performance-based teaching of Shakespeare is that by engaging students vocally, emotionally, and physically, it is then much easier to engage them intellectually because they are invested in the words, the characters, and the story. We always start on our feet, and later we sit and talk.

SIX ELEMENTS OF DRAMA: PLOT, CHARACTER, THEME, DICTION, MUSIC, AND SPECTACLE

Over two thousand years ago, Aristotle's *Poetics* outlined six elements of drama, in order of importance: Plot, Character, Theme, Diction, Music, and Spectacle. Because Shakespeare was foremost a playwright, it is helpful to take a brief look at these six elements as they relate to directing a Shakespeare play in the classroom.

PLOT (ACTION)

To Aristotle, plot was the most important element. One of the purposes of *The 30-Minute Shakespeare* is to provide a script that tells Shakespeare's stories, as opposed to concentrating on one scene. In a thirty-minute edit of a Shakespeare play, some plot elements are necessarily omitted. For the sake of a full understanding of the characters' relationships and motivations, it is helpful to make short plot summaries of each scene so that students are aware of their characters' arcs throughout the play. The scene descriptions in the Folger editions are sufficient to fill in the plot holes. Students can read the descriptions aloud during class time to ensure that the story is clear and that no plot elements are neglected. Additionally, there are one-page charts in the Folger editions of *Shakespeare Set Free*, indicating characters' relations graphically, with lines connecting families and factions to give students a visual representation of what can often be complex interrelationships, particularly in Shakespeare's history plays.

Young actors love action. That is why *The 30-Minute Shakespeare* includes dynamic blocking (stage direction) that allows students to tell the story in a physically dramatic fashion. Characters' movements on the stage are always motivated by the text itself.

CHARACTER

I consider myself a facilitator and a director more than an acting teacher. I want the students' understanding of their characters to spring from the text and the story. From there, I encourage them to consider how their character might talk, walk, stand, sit, eat, and drink. I also urge students to consider characters' motivations, objectives, and relationships, and I will ask pointed questions to that end during the rehearsal process. I try not to show the students how I would perform a scene, but if no ideas are forthcoming from anybody in the class, I will suggest a minimum of two possibilities for how the character might respond.

At times students may want more guidance and examples. Over thirteen years of directing plays in the classroom, I have wavered between wanting all the ideas to come from the students, and deciding that I need to be more of a "director," telling them what I would like to see them doing. It is a fine line, but in recent years I have decided that if I don't see enough dynamic action or characterization, I will step in and "direct" more. But I always make sure to leave room for students to bring themselves into the characters because their own ideas are invariably the best.

THEME (THOUGHTS, IDEAS)

In a typical English classroom, theme will be a big topic for discussion of a Shakespeare play. Using a performance-based method of teaching Shakespeare, an understanding of the play's themes develops from "mining the text" and exploring Shakespeare's words and his story. If the students understand what they are saying and how that relates to their characters and the overall story, the plays' themes will emerge clearly. We always return to the text itself. There are a number of elegant computer programs, such as www.wordle.net, that will count the number of recurring words in a passage and illustrate them graphically. For example, if the word "jealousy" comes up more than any other word in *Othello*, it will appear in a larger font. Seeing the words displayed by size in this way can offer up illuminating insights into the interaction between words in the text and the play's themes. Your computer-minded students might enjoy searching for such tidbits. There are more internet tools and websites in the Additional Resources section at the back of this book.

I cannot overstress the importance of acting out the play in understanding its themes. By embodying the roles of Othello and Iago and reciting their words, students do not simply comprehend the themes intellectually, but understand them kinesthetically, physically, and emotionally. They are essentially *living* the characters' jealousy, pride, and feelings about race. The themes of appearance vs.

reality, good vs. evil, honesty, misrepresentation, and self-knowledge (or lack thereof) become physically felt as well as intellectually understood. Performing Shakespeare delivers a richer understanding than that which comes from just reading the play. Students can now relate the characters' conflicts to their own struggles.

DICTION (LANGUAGE)

If I had to cite one thing I would like my actors to take from their experience of performing a play by William Shakespeare, it is an appreciation and understanding of the beauty of Shakespeare's language. The language is where it all begins and ends. Shakespeare's stories are dramatic, his characters are rich and complex, and his settings are exotic and fascinating, but it is through his language that these all achieve their richness. This leads me to spend more time on language than on any other element of the performance.

Starting with daily vocal warm-ups, many of them using parts of the script or other Shakespearean passages, I consistently emphasize the importance of the words. Young actors often lack experience in speaking clearly and projecting their voices outward, so in addition to comprehension, I emphasize projection, diction, breathing, pacing, dynamics, coloring of words, and vocal energy. *Theatre Games for Young Performers* contains many effective vocal exercises, as does the Folger's *Shakespeare Set Free* series. Consistent emphasis on all aspects of Shakespeare's language, especially on how to speak it effectively, is the most important element to any Shakespeare performance with a young cast.

MUSIC

A little music can go a long way in setting a mood for a thirty-minute Shakespeare play. I usually open the show with a short passage of music to set the tone. Thirty seconds of music played on a boom box operated by a student can provide a nice introduction to the play, create an atmosphere for the audience, and give the actors a sense of place and feeling.

iTunes is a good starting point for choosing your music. Typing in "Shakespeare" or "Hamlet" or "jealousy" (if you are going for a theme) will result in an excellent selection of aural performance enhancers at the very reasonable price of ninety-nine cents each (or free of charge, see Additional Resources section). Likewise, fight sounds, foreboding sounds, weather sounds (rain, thunder), trumpet sounds, etc. are all readily available online at affordable cost. I typically include three sound cues in a play, just enough to enhance but not overpower a production. The boom box operator sits on the far right or left of the stage, not backstage, so he can see the action. This also has the added benefit of having somebody out there with a script, capable of prompting in a pinch.

SPECTACLE

Aristotle considered spectacle the least important aspect of drama. Students tend to be surprised at this since we are used to being bombarded with production values on TV and video, often at the expense of substance. In my early days of putting on student productions, I would find myself hamstrung by my own ambitions in the realm of scenic design.

A simple bench or two chairs set on the stage are sufficient. The sense of "place" can be achieved through language and acting. Simple set dressing, a few key props, and some tasteful, emblematic costume pieces will go a long way toward providing all the "spectacle" you need.

In the stage directions to the plays in *The 30-Minute Shakespeare* series, I make frequent use of two large pillars stage left and right at the Folger Shakespeare Library's Elizabethan Theatre. I also have characters frequently entering and exiting from "stage rear." Your stage will have a different layout. Take a good look at the performing space you will be using and see if there are any elements that can be incorporated into your own stage directions. Is there a balcony? Can characters enter from the audience? (Make sure that they can get there from backstage, unless you want them waiting in the lobby until their entrance, which may be impractical.) If possible, make sure to rehearse in that space a few times to fix any technical issues and perhaps discover a few fun staging variations that will add pizzazz and dynamics to your own show.

The real spectacle is in the telling of the tale. Wooden swords are handy for characters that need them. Students should be warned at the outset that playing with swords outside of the scene is verboten. Letters, moneybags, and handkerchiefs should all have plentiful duplicates kept in a small prop box, as well as with a stage manager, because they tend to disappear in the hands of adolescents. After every rehearsal and performance, I recommend you personally sweep the rehearsal or performance area immediately for stray props. It is amazing what gets left behind.

Ultimately, the performances are about language and human drama, not set pieces, props, and special effects. Fake blood, glitter, glass, and liquids have no place on the stage; they are a recipe for disaster, or, at the very least, a big mess. On the other hand, the props that are employed can often be used effectively to convey character, as in Bardolph's aforementioned relationship with his wineskin.

PITFALLS AND SOLUTIONS

Putting on a play in a high school classroom is not easy. There are problems with enthusiasm, attitude, attention, and line memorization, to name a few. As anybody who has directed a play will tell you, it is always darkest before the dawn. My experience is that after one or two days of utter despair just before the play goes up, show day breaks and the play miraculously shines. To quote a recurring gag in one of my favorite movies, *Shakespeare in Love*: "It's a mystery."

ENTHUSIASM, FRUSTRATION, AND DISCIPLINE

Bring the enthusiasm yourself. Feed on the energy of the eager students, and others will pick up on that. Keep focused on the task at hand. Arrive prepared. Enthusiasm comes as you make headway. Ultimately, it helps to remind the students that a play is fun. I try to focus on the positive attributes of the students, rather than the ones that drive me crazy. This is easier said than done, but it is important. One season, I yelled at the group two days in a row. On day two of yelling, they tuned me out, and it took me a while to win them back. I learned my lesson; since then I've tried not to raise my voice out of anger or frustration. As I grow older and more mature, it is important for me to lead by example. It has been years since I yelled at a student group. If I am disappointed in their work or their behavior, I will express my disenchantment in words, speaking from the heart as somebody who cares about them and cares about our performance and our experience together. I find that fundamentally, young people want to please, to do well, and to be liked. If there is a serious discipline problem, I will hand it over to the regular classroom teacher, the administrator, or the parent.

LINE MEMORIZATION

Students may have a hard time memorizing lines. In these cases, see if you can pair them up with a "buddy" and existing friend who will run lines with them in person or over the phone after school. If students do not have such a "buddy," I volunteer to run lines with them myself. If serious line memorization problems arise that cannot be solved through work, then two students can switch parts if it is early enough in the rehearsal process. For doubled roles, the scene with fewer lines can go to the actor who is having memorization problems. Additionally, a few passages or lines can be cut. Again, it is important to address these issues early. Later cuts become more problematic as other actors have already memorized their cues. I have had to do late cuts about twice in thirteen years. While they have gotten us out of jams, it is best to assess early whether a student will have line memorization problems, and deal with the problem sooner rather than later.

In production, always keep several copies of the script backstage, as well as cheat sheets indicating cues, entrances, and scene changes. Make a prop list, indicating props for each scene, as well as props that are the responsibility of individual actors. Direct the Stage Manager and an Assistant Stage Manager to keep track of these items, and on show days, personally double-check if you can.

In thirteen years of preparing an inner-city public high school English class for a public performance on a field trip to the Folger Secondary School Shakespeare Festival, my groups and I have been beset by illness, emotional turmoil, discipline problems, stage fright, adolescent angst, midlife crises (not theirs), and all manner of other emergencies, including acts of God and nature. Despite the difficulties and challenges inherent in putting on a Shakespeare play with a group of young people, one amazing fact stands out in my experience. Here is how many times a student has been absent for show day: Zero. Somehow, everybody has always made it to the show, and the show has gone on. How can this be? It's a mystery.

✳ PERFORMANCE NOTES: *TWELFTH NIGHT*

Twelfth Night is my favorite Shakespeare play. I love the current of bittersweet longing that runs below the surface of this comedy. The characters of Feste, Maria, Malvolio, Sir Toby Belch, Sir Andrew Aguecheek, Olivia, and Viola are full of charm and depth. The language, the relationships, and the songs paint a theatrical picture that is at once merry and melancholy.

This production was my first outing as a high school play director, working under the auspices of the Folger Library, and the only time in my fourteen-year Teaching Artist residency that I worked with eleventh graders. I was lucky to have a group of students who threw themselves into the project, joyfully occupying some of Shakespeare's richest characters.

I directed this performance of *Twelfth Night* in 1997. These notes are the result of my own review of the performance video. They are not intended to be the "definitive" performance notes for all productions of *Twelfth Night.* Your production will be unique to you and your cast. That is the magic of live theater. What is interesting about these notes is that many of the performance details I mention were not part of the original stage directions. They either emerged spontaneously on performance day or were developed by students in rehearsal after the stage directions had been written into the script. Some of these pieces of stage business work like a charm. Others fall flat. Still others are unintentionally hilarious. My favorites are the ones that arise directly from the students themselves and demonstrate a union between actor and character, as if that individual becomes a vehicle for the character he is playing. To witness a sixteen-year-old young man "become" Feste as Shakespeare's words leave his mouth is a memorable moment indeed.

The actor who played Feste in this production possessed a natural joy and physical looseness that captivated the audience and garnered him a major award at the Folger Library Secondary School Shakespeare Festival. He moved about the stage with the lilting grace of a basketball player and delivered his lines with a winning grin. Occasionally one has the fortune to encounter someone whose innate charm fills a room. Such was this unforgettable Feste.

SCENE 1 (ACT I, SCENE V)

As the narrator introduces the roles, each actor crosses the stage in character and exits. This technique offers a fitting preview of the players and sets a merry tone. Sir Toby stumbles onto the bench (with a "fat-pillow" under his shirt), offers his mug to the narrator, who declines, and then falls to the floor. The narrator turns to look at him and then back to the audience, expressionless. The action gets a laugh and immediately breaks the fourth wall by bringing the narrator into the story as a character. Sir Andrew Aguecheek drags Sir Toby offstage by his feet. Maria dusts the table, and Feste dances a little jig, then hides behind the stage right pillar. Right away the audience sees what kinds of people populate this colorful comedy.

By a stroke of great luck, not only did the student who played Feste overflow with charisma, but he also juggled! On the line, "Those that are fools, let them use their talents," he performed a bit of three-ball juggling with a fancy finish and was met with enthusiastic applause. If your Feste does not juggle, he can balance an ostrich feather, flip a hat onto his head, or do a handstand or somersault. Or he can perform a long build-up to a "nothing trick." Feste's real talent is his wit.

The actor also contributed his own physicalizations. On "God bless you, Lady," he slid on his knees toward Olivia. Raising the physical stakes sheds light on character traits and relationships. Later, when Feste is leaning on the handle of a broom, Malvolio is directed to knock the broom with his cane, causing Feste to fall. In rehearsal Malvolio pushed Feste to the floor instead, and we kept it for the performance. This is a crueler action that casts a small shadow over the light comedy. Importantly, it draws the battle lines between Malvolio and the revelers, which justifies his cruel comeuppance later in the play.

Feste exits the stage in the first scene while bobbing, weaving, and flapping his elbows. He looks like a boxing chicken! Playing "animal essences" is a good way for actors to explore the more primal elements of their characters. The rooster has long been a symbol of the Fool, so Feste's chicken dance is an apt choice—and one that is his choice, not mine as director. The best choices often come from the actors themselves. Our job as directors is to foster an atmosphere where creative experimentation can flourish.

The meeting between Viola and Olivia provides another opportunity for actors to find actions that bring Shakespeare's text to life. Olivia turns her back to Viola to remove her veil, looks in a hand-held mirror, and touches up her makeup. This sequence dovetails nicely with Viola's subsequent line, "Excellently done, if God did all." By mining the text, and experimenting with movements and speech interpretations, young performers discover the full richness of this beautiful work. Sometimes a subtle change in delivery can generate audience laughter. For example, Viola pauses after the words "Excellently done" and Olivia responds with a flattered giggle. When Viola adds "if God did all," Olivia's giggle changes into flustered embarrassment.

After Viola's beautiful "Make me a willow cabin at your gate" speech, Olivia puts her hand to her chest and gulps. Her eyes bug out, which gets a good laugh. Olivia then aggressively comes toward Viola with her arms outstretched and backs her into the pillar. Viola ducks and escapes. This sequence is not only very funny, but it also demonstrates the power dynamic between Olivia and Viola. Olivia is clearly the dominant character and aggressor. As the lady of the house, she is in power. Viola is but a messenger. Through movement and vocal choices, the actors are clarifying their social status.

We have fun with Viola's attempts to disguise herself as a man. Viola clears her throat before the line "I am a gentleman" in order to speak in a lower pitch. This works best when she first briefly forgets to disguise her high-pitched voice (in the heat of her impassioned speech). By forgetting, then remembering, that she is disguising herself as a man, Viola adds comedy, dramatic tension, and pathos, particularly in her scenes with the Duke.

Like the young man playing Feste, the actress playing Olivia in this production had a knack for comic physical mannerisms. In her speech praising Cesario's (Viola's) qualities, she performed a lusty pelvic gyration, to the delight of the audience. This move sprung organically from her. She brought Shakespeare's words to her character and became Olivia in the throes of passion. Olivia repeats the same move more fluidly on the line "Well, let it be." Recurrence of a physical action reinforces it as a character's mannerism, rather than an isolated "bit," and repetition enhances comedy (especially in threes).

SCENE 2 (ACT II, SCENE IV)

Sometimes a performer makes a surprising choice. In this production of *Twelfth Night,* the young woman playing the part of Curio decided that her character was gay. There is plenty of cross-dressing and gender bending in the play, and the scenes between both Orsino/Viola and Antonio/Sebastian have distinctly homoerotic overtones. There is nothing in the text to suggest overtly that Curio is gay, but she made a strong commitment to her portrayal. The decision informed how she dressed, stood, moved, and even ate an apple.

Curio is a small role, with only two lines in this adaptation. I appreciate how this actor created an inner world for her character that imparted a humanness and dimensionality to the whole scene.

Frequently young performers believe their smaller roles are unimportant, but this flashy Curio proved otherwise.

Likewise the two musicians in this scene, a flute player and a melodica player, provide comic relief. Every time the melodica player tries to play a note, she is interrupted, first by the flute player, then by the drummers, to her increasing frustration. The old theatre adage is true: "There are no small parts, only small actors."

There are three songs in the production, each one distinct and beautiful. "Come Away Death" features a roving rap troupe that enters to accompany Feste, complete with drumming and fist bumps. The call-and-response vocals and unison dance moves bring the energy to a fever pitch, and the piece ends with Feste on his knees across the front of the group, arms akimbo, flashing peace signs with his hands. The audience erupts in sustained applause. This is what it means to "own" a Shakespeare play.

SCENE 3 (ACT II, SCENE III)

The music in *Twelfth Night* provides much of the play's magic, merriment, and melancholy. In 1997, the actress playing Maria sang "O Mistress Mine" a capella, as the tavern revelers behind her gently swayed to the music. Rare is the student actor who chooses to sing a song solo with no instrumental accompaniment, and this Maria succeeded with aplomb. The production featured all live music (nothing prerecorded), adding spark and vitality to the show.

In this final scene, as tavern revelers Sir Toby, Andrew Aguecheek, and Feste encircle the table banging on pots and chanting, the drummer from Feste's band joins the crew. When Malvolio comes in to silence the late-night caterwauling, the drummer, engrossed in the music, plays a drum solo. Malvolio grabs the musician's drumstick and breaks it over his knee, to which the audience responds vocally. Without missing a beat, the drummer grabs another stick from his coat and continues playing, to the delight of the spectators.

Feste's Song ("Wind and Rain") closes this spirited *Twelfth Night*. The entire cast sings the song, with Feste spurring the audience to rhythmic clapping while skipping around the assembled players. The magic of Shakespeare transforms an eleventh grade English class into a troupe of consummate thespians, musicians, comedians, and moving tale-tellers. They provide a rollicking and heartfelt finish to my favorite Shakespeare play; may it touch your heart too. Using this book as a guideline, I hope the experience of performing this beautiful, bittersweet comedy will bring delight and laughter to actors, educators, and audiences alike.

✳ *TWELFTH NIGHT:* SET AND PROP LIST

SET PIECES:

Bench
Table
Three chairs
Throne

PROPS:

SCENE 1:
Mirror, makeup kit and brush
Cleaning cloth and broom
Bottle of wine
Two wine glasses
Change purse, coin, and ring
Juggling balls
Scroll of paper
Veils for Olivia and Attendants

SCENE 2:
Bottle of wine
Two wine glasses
Bowl of fruit
Musical instruments (flute and trumpet or equivalent)
Mirror
Drums

SCENE 3:
Mugs
Bottles
Pots and pans
Wooden spoons
Flask
Money purse
Nightshirt, nightcap, and slippers
Drum and two drumsticks

BANNEKER HIGH SCHOOL *presents*

Twelfth Night
By William Shakespeare

April 16, 1997
Instructor: Mrs. Brenda Jones | Director: Mr. Nick Newlin

CAST OF CHARACTERS:
In order of appearance

Act I, Scene 5. A courtyard at Countess Olivia's estate.

Narrator: Nicole Thompson
Feste, *Countess Olivia's jester:* Aaron Jenkins
Maria, *Olivia's waiting-gentlewoman:* Melissa Moffett
Olivia, *an Illyrian countess:* Keonna Carter
Viola, *a lady of Messaline shipwrecked on the coast of Illyria (disguised as Cesario):*
  Rasheeda Mullings
Malvolio, *steward in Olivia's household:* Jese Gary
Attendants *to Olivia:* Michelle Deal, Maya Young

Act II, Scene 4. At the court of the Duke Orsino.

Narrator: Monica Thomas
Orsino, *Duke of Illyria:* Geri Averytt
Curio, *gentleman serving Orsino:* Latori Patton
Viola: Raquel Diaz
Orsino's Band: Flute: Khalia Spivey. **Violin:** Janesia A. Geter. **Melodica:** Michelle Deal.
Feste's Band: Aaron Jenkins, Jamaal R. Grimes *(drums)*, Derek Rucker *(drums)*, et al.

Act II, Scene 3. The kitchen at Countess Olivia's estate.

Narrator: Michelle Deal
Sir Toby Belch, *Olivia's kinsman:* Alexandria Carroll
Sir Andrew Aguecheek, *Sir Toby's companion:* Charles McCants
Maria: Melissa Moffett
Feste: Aaron Jenkins
Malvolio: Jese Gary
Feste's Band: Aaron Jenkins, Jamaal R. Grimes *(drums)*, Derek Rucker *(drums)*
Singers: Melissa Moffett, Laura Bibbs, Maya Young, Latori Patton, Raquel Diaz

Stage Manager: Calvin Wingfield
Stage Crew: Calvin Wingfield, Derek Rucker, Laura Bibbs, Danielle Jones
Costumes: Danielle Jones
Technical: Jamaal R. Grimes
Sets and Props: Khalia Spivey

ADDITIONAL RESOURCES

SHAKESPEARE

Shakespeare Set Free: Teaching Romeo and Juliet, Macbeth and a Midsummer Night's Dream
Peggy O'Brien, Ed., Teaching Shakespeare Institute
Washington Square Press
New York, 1993

Shakespeare Set Free: Teaching Hamlet and Henry IV, Part 1
Peggy O'Brien, Ed., Teaching Shakespeare Institute
Washington Square Press
New York, 1994

Shakespeare Set Free: Teaching Twelfth Night and Othello
Peggy O'Brien, Ed., Teaching Shakespeare Institute
Washington Square Press
New York, 1995

The *Shakespeare Set Free* series is an invaluable resource with lesson plans, activites, handouts, and excellent suggestions for rehearsing and performing Shakespeare plays in a classroom setting.

ShakesFear and How to Cure It!
Ralph Alan Cohen
Prestwick House, Inc.
Delaware, 2006

The Friendly Shakespeare:
A Thoroughly Painless Guide to the Best of the Bard
Norrie Epstein
Penguin Books
New York, 1994

Brush Up Your Shakespeare!
Michael Macrone
Cader Books
New York, 1990

Shakespeare's Insults:
Educating Your Wit
Wayne F. Hill and Cynthia J. Ottchen
Three Rivers Press
New York, 1991

Practical Approaches to Teaching Shakespeare
Peter Reynolds
Oxford University Press
New York, 1991

Scenes From Shakespeare:
A Workbook for Actors
Robin J. Holt
McFarland and Co.
London, 1988

THEATER AND PERFORMANCE

Impro: Improvisation and the Theatre
Keith Johnstone
Routledge Books
London, 1982

A Dictionary of Theatre Anthropology:
The Secret Art of the Performer
Eugenio Barba and Nicola Savarese
Routledge
London, 1991

THEATER GAMES

Theatre Games for Young Performers
Maria C. Novelly
Meriwether Publishing
Colorado, 1990

Improvisation for the Theater
Viola Spolin
Northwestern University Press
Illinois, 1983

Theater Games for Rehearsal:
A Director's Handbook
Viola Spolin
Northwestern University Press
Illinois, 1985

101 Theatre Games for Drama
Teachers, Classroom Teachers
& Directors
Mila Johansen
Players Press Inc.
California, 1994

PLAY DIRECTING

Theater and the Adolescent Actor:
Building a Successful School Program
Camille L. Poisson
Archon Books
Connecticut, 1994

Directing for the Theatre
W. David Sievers
Wm. C. Brown, Co.
Iowa, 1965

The Director's Vision: Play Direction
from Analysis to Production
Louis E. Catron
Mayfield Publishing Co.
California, 1989

INTERNET RESOURCES

http://www.folger.edu
The Folger Shakespeare Library's
website has lesson plans, primary
sources, study guides, images,
workshops, programs for teachers
and students, and much more. The
definitive Shakespeare website for
educators, historians and all lovers
of the Bard.

http://www.shakespeare.mit.edu.
The Complete Works of
William Shakespeare.
All complete scripts for *The
30-Minute Shakespeare* series were
originally downloaded from this site
before editing. Links to other internet
resources.

http://www.LoMonico.com/
Shakespeare-and-Media.htm
http://shakespeare-and-media
.wikispaces.com
Michael LoMonico is Senior
Consultant on National Education
for the Folger Shakespeare Library.
His *Seminar Shakespeare 2.0* offers a
wealth of information on how to use
exciting new approaches and online
resources for teaching Shakespeare.

http://www.freesound.org.
A collaborative database of sounds
and sound effects.

http://www.wordle.net.
A program for creating "word clouds"
from the text that you provide. The
clouds give greater prominence to
words that appear more frequently in
the source text.

http://www.opensourceshakespeare
.org.
This site has good searching capacity.

http://shakespeare.palomar.edu/
default.htm
Excellent links and searches

http://shakespeare.com/
Write like Shakespeare,
Poetry Machine, tag cloud

http://www.shakespeare-online.com/

http://www.bardweb.net/

http://www.rhymezone.com/
shakespeare/
Good searchable word and phrase
finder.
Or by lines:
http://www.rhymezone.com/
shakespeare/toplines/

http://shakespeare.mcgill.ca/
Shakespeare and Performance
research team

http://www.enotes.com/william-
shakespeare

Needless to say, the internet goes on and on with valuable Shakespeare resources.
The ones listed here are excellent starting points and will set you on your way in the
great adventure that is Shakespeare.

NICK NEWLIN has performed a comedy and variety act for international audiences for twenty-seven years. Since 1996, he has conducted an annual play directing residency affiliated with the Folger Shakespeare Library in Washington, D.C. Newlin received a BA with Honors from Harvard University in 1982 and an MA in Theater with an emphasis in Play Directing from the University of Maryland in 1996.

THE 30-MINUTE SHAKESPEARE

A MIDSUMMER NIGHT'S DREAM
978-1-935550-00-6

ROMEO AND JULIET
978-1-935550-01-3

MUCH ADO ABOUT NOTHING
978-1-935550-03-7

MACBETH
978-1-935550-02-0

THE MERRY WIVES OF WINDSOR
978-1-935550-05-1

TWELFTH NIGHT
978-1-935550-04-4

AVAILABLE IN FALL 2010

AS YOU LIKE IT
978-1-935550-06-8

LOVE'S LABOR'S LOST
978-1-935550-07-5

THE COMEDY OF ERRORS
978-1-935550-08-2

KING LEAR
978-1-935550-09-9

HENRY IV, PART 1
978-1-935550-11-2

OTHELLO
978-1-935550-10-5

All plays $7.95, available in bookstores everywhere

"Nick Newlin's 30-minute play cuttings are perfect for students who have no experience with Shakespeare. Each 30-minute mini-play is a play in itself with a beginning, middle, and end." —Michael Ellis-Tolaydo, Department of Theater, Film, and Media Studies, St Mary's College of Maryland